305.896 M648a
MILLER
AN APPEAL TO C

3.50

WITHDRAWN

Library

5801 Wilson Avenue
St. Louis, Missouri 63110

THE AMERICAN NEGRO
HIS HISTORY AND LITERATURE

AN APPEAL TO CONSCIENCE

Kelly Miller

11-18-69

ARNO PRESS and THE NEW YORK TIMES
NEW YORK 1969

Copyright © 1969 by Arno Press, Inc.
All rights reserved

*

Library of Congress Catalog Card No. 69–18553

*

Reprinted from a copy in the collection of
Harvard College Library

*

Manufactured in the United States of America

General Editor
WILLIAM LOREN KATZ

KELLY MILLER, DEAN OF THE COLLEGE OF Liberal Arts at Howard University, was a sociologist and prolific essayist whose fertile and lucid pen mirrored much of the thinking of American Negroes during the first third of the twentieth century. Miller reached manhood toward the end of the nineteenth century, at a time of increasing racial proscription and degradation. It was a period of disfranchisement and Jim Crow laws in the South, of sharecropping for the majority of black men who lived in the rural South; of the apogee in the numbers of lynchings and of increasing race riots in both North and South; of growing indifference or hostility to Negroes on the part of the white North.

Accordingly, the early twentieth century was a time when accommodation—epitomized in the philosophy and leadership of Booker T. Washington—gained the upper hand in Negro thought and action. It was also a period when a small band of articulate intellectuals, led by W. E. B. DuBois, expressed a philosophy of protest that gained the ascendancy after the First World War. Miller, reflecting a broad spectrum of thought among the Negro middle and upper classes, stood between the two men, attempting to synthesize elements from the thought of both; he was, contemporaries said —and he himself conceded—"a straddler." Yet as currents in Negro ideologies moved from a mood of extreme discouragements and accommodation around 1900, to greater militance during World War I and after, Miller likewise progressed to the left—all the while remaining a pragmatic harmonizer of the conservative and radical wings of Negro thought, and an adroit appellant to both the conscience and benevolence of the white American reading public.

An Appeal to Conscience exemplifies Miller's thought at this juncture—at the end of World War I, when Negroes were becoming more militant, and when whites were ideologically committed to a war to "save the world for democracy." His book is a judicious, reasoned, measured appeal to the American white man's conscience to do justice to the black man. It protests firmly but moderately. It concedes the weak position of the American Negro—and skillfully compares it to that of the

Belgian victims of the German invasion, for whom white America had shed many tears. Miller rests his case upon the values in the American Democratic Creed—a creed that white Americans thought they were defending and advancing during the Great War.

The irony, of course, was that at no time since the Civil War had the gap between the American creed and actual reality been greater. President Woodrow Wilson, who combined racist attitudes with a deep concern for democratic values, epitomized that contradiction. Under the circumstances, the mainstream of Negro protest tended to be mild—a tendency reinforced by the pressures for conformity and the Attorney General's invasion of civil liberties that characterized this World War I period. Accordingly, a protest organization like the NAACP, founded in 1909, carried on its campaign of propaganda and litigation while urging Negroes to be patriotic, support the war effort, and hope to benefit from the predicted advance of democracy in the postwar years. Protest tended, therefore, to be moderate and reasonable, rather than strident, in its appeal to the white man's conscience. To the far left of both Miller and the NAACP, A. Philip Randolph, editor of the *Messenger* magazine, did denounce the war as an imperialist venture, and he vigorously denounced American racism (while at the same time denouncing W. E. B. DuBois and the NAACP for their more moderate policy), and was nearly jailed for sedition.

Miller, though his tone was more conciliatory toward the whites than was that of the early NAACP, basically reflected a similar tactic and point of view—emphasizing the loyalty and patriotism of the black man, while calling for a redress of grievances, in his appeal to the white man's conscience. To most articulate Negroes of that period—including the noted W. E. B. DuBois, editor of the NAACP's *Crisis* magazine, it seemed that, given the dual content of the demand for loyalty and patriotism on the one hand, and the intensive propaganda regarding the preservation of democracy on the other—both of which were occasioned by the war—this was the strategy calculated to most likely produce an easing of the black man's burden in the United States. The virtue of Mr. Miller's essays in this volume is that they sum up this viewpoint with such felicity.

August Meier
DEPARTMENT OF HISTORY
KENT STATE UNIVERSITY

AN APPEAL TO CONSCIENCE

THE MACMILLAN COMPANY
NEW YORK · BOSTON · CHICAGO · DALLAS
ATLANTA · SAN FRANCISCO

MACMILLAN & CO., LIMITED
LONDON · BOMBAY · CALCUTTA
MELBOURNE

THE MACMILLAN CO. OF CANADA, LTD.
TORONTO

AN APPEAL TO CONSCIENCE

America's Code of Caste
A Disgrace to Democracy

BY

KELLY MILLER
Dean of the College of Arts and Sciences
of Howard University, Washington

WITH AN INTRODUCTION BY

ALBERT BUSHNELL HART

New York
THE MACMILLAN COMPANY
1918

All rights reserved

Copyright, 1918
By THE MACMILLAN COMPANY

Set up and electrotyped. Published June, 1918.

TO

RIGHT MINDED AMERICA

"Ring out false pride in place and blood,
The civil slander and the spite;
Ring in the love of truth and right,
Ring in the common love of good."

INTRODUCTION

PROFESSOR MILLER raises in this book the question to which a solution has never yet been found. How is it possible to reconcile in the United States of America a system of discriminations against a race which counts a tenth of the population, with the great national principles of equality of opportunity and civil and political rights for the remaining nine-tenths? The most candid and sympathetic reader may therefore find some of the author's positions out of focus with previous observations. For instance, while cordially appreciating the work and its spirit, it is not essential to accept the author's dictum that "a physical and spiritual identity of all peoples occupying common territory is a logical necessity of thought." The book is written with excellent temper and an admission of difficulties which are very deep seated if not irremovable. The main thesis is a protest against the application of one standard to black men and another to white men. That such a discrimination exists is clear, and the evil consequences are well set forth.

The chapter on Lawlessness is a just though spirited protest against lynching, an offence which does the white race ten times as much harm as the negroes, for it brutalizes the law-making and law-applying section of the population. It thrusts down the white farmer or townsman or working-man to a level below that of the worst negro criminal, because the lyncher glories in his crime. The chapter on Segregation exposes the brutality and uselessness of Jim Crow Laws and might go further by pointing out that there is never any segregation of negro purchasers who have the money to buy from white salesmen and store-keepers.

The main thesis is summed up in the chapter on Righteousness. Professor Miller does not in the least deny that the presence of the two races side by side brings difficulties and jealousies for which neither side is primarily responsible. What he does insist upon is that the principles of justice, impartiality and fair dealing, the relation of morals to conduct, rightly apply as much to men of negro blood as to other races, and should especially be observed by the whites in relation to the negroes. It all goes back to Emerson's great saying, "If I put a chain upon a slave, I fix the other end around my own neck." The book is a powerful appeal to the dominant race to protect itself by a fair treatment of the unorganized race. As the author puts it, "Prosperity will take no pride in the deeds of this day which deprive the humblest citizen of his human rights in order that others may enjoy a larger measure of easement."

Kelly Miller is a disputant of proof.

INTRODUCTION

It is not necessary to agree with everything he says in order to find common ground. Some arguments and some illustrations might be left out without weakening his case. The merit of the book is its vigorous and well stated appeal to reason, a call for a just application of the moral principles of which America is proud. It is a logical, human, reasonable appeal to the doctrines of Christianity and of democracy, of which the nation is so proud. Its motto might well be "Physician heal thyself."

ALBERT BUSHNELL HART.

CONTENTS

AN APPEAL TO CONSCIENCE

CHAPTER I

RACE CONTACT

THE contact, adjustment and attrition of the various races of mankind constitute the gravest problem of modern civilization. This problem is not limited by local or national boundaries; is not confined to continental or hemispheric divisions of the earth's surface; but is world wide in its scope and operation. The conflict of races is the dominating problem of Europe, Asia, Africa, Australia, North and South America, and the scattered islands of the seas. The political and economic issues which now threaten disruption of the foundation of social order, on deeper analysis, will be found to have their root in the deeper issue of race.

In the United States we have but an infinitesimal fraction of the universal race problem; and yet, the American Negro problem presents certain unique and peculiar features which cause the students of social subjects to bestow upon it a degree of attention accorded to no other point of race contact throughout the globe. Among these peculiar features may be mentioned: (1) In the United States we have the most gigantic instance in history where the weaker race has been brought into the territory of the stronger as a servile element. The stronger race usually overruns the territory of the weaker, reduces it to subjection, and imposes upon the subdued people its lordly *régime*. (2) The Negro and the European represent widely divergent ethnic types. The experiment of adjusting markedly different races on terms of equality, under democratic institutions, is here being tried for the first time in the history of race relationship. The weaker element is greatly outnumbered by the stronger, and is unevenly distributed over the geographical area. The numerical inferiority of the Negro renders his presence less menaceful in the judgment of the more populous and more powerful race; while his segregation in the South produces a state of unbalanced pressure of public sentiment concerning his place and part in the general political and social scheme. The traditional attitude of the North and the South grows out of this unevenness of numerical distribution.

The United States thus becomes the world's most interesting laboratory for working out the intricate issues of race adjustment. Well might the social philosopher observe with keenest interest this tremendous experiment; for, if this experiment succeeds, it will furnish a sure criterion for the solution of the various race problems which are coterminous with the ends of the earth.

Voltaire, the famous French philosopher, states that it is more difficult and more meritorious to civilize the barbarian than it is to wean men from their prejudices. Here we have the dual nature of the race problem expressed in the clear terms of a French aphorism. How can the white race be freed of prejudice while the Negro is being lifted to the level of surrounding civilization? Either of these problems is sufficient to tax human ingenuity. But when we roll the two into one, the world stands bewildered at the task. To add to its bewilderment, these two features seem to be incompatible, the one with the other. The more progressive and ambitious the Negro becomes, the less tolerable he seems to be to his white lord and master. The good old Negro slave who was ever faithful and loyal to the welfare of his lord and master was always acceptable to him. But his more ambitious son, with a college diploma in his knapsack, is *persona non grata.* The Negro coachman can drive his white master to the depot, sitting side by side and cheek by jowl, with complaisant satisfaction; but a different situation is created should they become joint occupants of a settee in a railway coach, where each pays his own fare and rides on terms of equality.

The attitude of the white race towards the Negro must be accounted for in the light of the origin of their relationship. The Negro was brought to this country for the purpose of performing manual and menial labor. No more account was taken of his higher susceptibilities than of the higher faculties of the lower animals. His function was supposed to be as purely mechanical as that of the ox who pulls the plough. There was no more thought of incorporating him into the body social than of thus ennobling the beasts of burden. The institution of slavery made no requisition upon the higher human faculties of the Negro, and, consequently, its philosophers denied their existence. Those who assumed not only the goodness, but also the piety of their day and generation, at one time stoutly denied that the Negro possessed a soul to be saved; and he was, therefore, refused the rite of Christian baptism. And then the wise ones declared that he did not possess an intellect that could be enlightened after the European formulas. They said that the Negro's skull was too thick to learn, and, in order to make the prediction work out its own fulfilment, they forthwith passed laws forbidding the attempt. What nature decreed he could not do, man declared he should not try. It is always an indication of uncertainty of thought and disquietude of conscience when men begin to re-enact the laws of the Almighty. The institution of African slavery sought to exploit the Negro's utility as a tool, in utter disregard of his higher human qualities. The Negro has had to fight his way upward from this low level of valuation of his animal and mechanical powers to a just appraisement of his intellectual, moral and spiritual endowments which differentiate him from the brute creation. The one clear ray of hope of the ultimate satisfactory adjustment of the races is seen in the fuller degree of recognition which the unfolding human faculties of the Negro command from an unwilling world. The superiority of the black man's spiritual endowment is now universally conceded. Whether or not his skull is less thick than formerly, no one now affects to doubt his ability to learn, except those who themselves need to be pitied for their incapacity to grasp the truth. On final analysis, it will be found that it is not flesh and blood, but intellectual, moral and spiritual qualities that constitute the controlling factor in human relationship.

The earlier philosophers of Negro subordination maintained, with infallible dogma, that the Negro was inherently and unalterably inferior in human qualities as a part of God's cosmic scheme of things. This inferiority of nature was assumed to be ample justification for all the treatment which was bestowed upon him. But the progress of events plays havoc with preconceived notions. Inferiority and superiority are relative and temporary terms. The rapidly developing powers and faculties of the Negro are making all but the infallible sceptical concerning the basis of their philosophy. It is interesting to note how these philosophers of Negro subordination have been compelled to shift from one discredited theory to another, like a frightened bird that flutters and flits from twig to twig, as they bend and break beneath its tremulous weight. There seems to be a touch of primeval jealousy which is always fearful of the under man, lest he stretch forth his hand and partake of the tree of civilization and eat and live and become as one of us. The fear is well founded. It is only a comprehensive knowledge of human welfare that frees us from fear.

Those who reason thus tell us that this is a white man's civilization. Because the Negro has no clearly traceable historical connection with this civilization, they tell us that it is none of his. But they forget the moral of that Scripture parable in which the laborer coming into the vineyard at the eleventh hour was received in terms of compensatory equality with those who had borne the heat and burden of the day. Other men have labored, and we have entered into their labors. The white race today is in the forefront of the civilized movements of the world. They are the trustees of civilization, and, if true to their trust, it must be administered not only for the

welfare of their own breed after the flesh, but for all of the sons and daughters of men. Like all of the higher values of life, civilization will die unless it is propagated among all who are capable of embracing it. In *Romeo and Juliet,* Shakespeare has stated the self-enlarging law of human affection—the more I give, the more I have. Universal law is reversible; it is as true when stated backward as when stated forward. The less of the higher values we give, the less we have. If an individual tries to keep his religion to himself, he will soon have no religion. And so it is with the higher form of civilization and culture.

The attitude of the white mind towards the Negro is understandable in the light of the former relationship of master and slave. The normal human attitude is conservative and resents alteration and change. We do not like to see our erstwhile inferior assume equality. It is expecting, perhaps, too much of human nature, to suppose that the southern white man would accept with satisfaction of feeling a sudden transformation of the slave into the freeman, or of a former inferior into an equal. We must await the propitiating element of time to assuage the animosities and bias of mind engendered by ages of asserted and accepted dogma.

To bolster up the cherished dogma, it is declared that race prejudice is a natural antipathy, and, therefore, is not subject to regulation and control. Henry W. Grady, not only the mouthpiece, but the oracle of the South, declared in one of his deliverances, that he believed that natural instinct would hold the races asunder, but, if such instinct did not exist, he would strengthen race prejudice so as to make it hold the stubbornness and strength of instinct. Analysis of the nature and theory of race prejudice would lead too far into the realm of philosophic speculation for the purposes of the present undertaking. It is sufficient to say, however, that the criterion of an instinctive characteristic is tested by its modifiability. A quality that is easily modified is not considered the product of heredity, but the acquisition of environment. Race prejudice is stronger on the part of the white race in Richmond, Virginia, than it is in Boston, Massachusetts. It is stronger in the United States today than it was a generation ago. It is immeasurably stronger in the adult than in the child. Its manifestations on the part of the same individual, under the same stimulus, varies with time, place and circumstances. The Civil War suddenly raised the thermometer of public feeling to such a degree that it seemed, for a time, that, on the part of many individuals, race prejudice would be wiped out altogether. The intensity of race feeling is proportionate to the number of Negroes in the community. Race prejudice takes on a different form of manifestation in communities where slavery once existed and in those communities where it did not prevail. If race antipathy is a natural endowment, it would, necessarily, be reciprocal in its operation. It is not claimed that it asserts itself on the part of the Negro against the white man, but always in the opposite direction. It is sometimes asserted that the Negro seeks unwarranted association with the white race, in preference to his own blood relation. If true, this assertion would destroy the foundation upon which belief in innate race antagonism rests. It shows that the desire for contact with superior attainment early nullifies whatever stubbornness and strength the assumed antipathy of race may possess. And thus, in various ways, it is clearly manifest that the feeling which we call race prejudice is profoundly modifiable by time, circumstance and condition. It is equally clear that whatever inherency it may possess, it is sufficiently controllable to permit the Negro to enjoy the full and free exercise of his rights and prerogatives as a citizen in a democratic republic.

We may as well dismiss without argument the various theories of the outcome of race contact as being inapplicable to the present situation. It is merely necessary to mention extermination and expulsion to prove their self-absurdity. Absorption of the Negro by the white race is too remote to be considered as a practicable proposition. I may be permitted to repeat here what I have said elsewhere:

"It must be taken for granted in the final outcome of things that the color line will be wholly obliterated. While blood may be thicker than water, it does not possess the spissitude or inherency of everlasting principle. The brotherhood of man is more fundamental than the fellowship of race. A physical and spiritual identity of all peoples occupying common territory is a logical necessity of thought. The clear seeing mind refuses to yield or give its assent to any other ultimate conclusion. This consummation, however, is far too removed from the sphere of present probability to have decisive influence upon practical procedure. It runs parallel with the prophecy that every valley shall be exalted and every hill shall be brought low. This is a physical necessity. Under the continuing law of gravitation, every stream that trickles down the mountain side, every downpour of rain, and every passing gust of wind removes infinite particles and shifts them from a higher to a lower level. This tendency to lower the one and lift the other will continue everlastingly until equality has been established as the final condition of stable equilibrium. In the meantime, however, the human race must adjust itself to the existence of mountain and valley as a lasting, if not everlasting, reality. Likewise, perpetual attrition of races must ultimately wear away all distinction and result in a universal blend. But the approximation of this goal is too slow and imperceptible to have any effect upon the present plan of race adjustment. We are concerned with persistent, stubborn realities which we have the power neither to influence nor affect, and must deal with conditions as they are in our day and generation, and not as we may vainly or vaguely imagine them in the ages yet to be." . . .

The two races will continue to exist side by side. They are linked to a common destiny of good or evil and their relations should be characterized by amity rather than by enmity. The Negro appeals to the white race in the language of Ruth to Naomi:

"Entreat me not to leave thee, or to return from following after thee: for whither thou goest, I will go; and where thou lodgest, I will lodge; thy people shall be my people, and thy God my God. Where thou diest will I die, and there will I be buried."

CHAPTER II

LAWLESSNESS

THE spirit of lawlessness against the Negro culminates in the practice of lynching. The whole civilized world is frequently shocked at the horrible lynchings of human beings such as took place at Waco, Memphis and East St. Louis. These horrible happenings are but eruptive symptoms of the race problem which break forth ever and anon with Vesuvian violence. These periodic outbreaks of lawlessness are but the outgrowth of the disfavor and despite in which the Negro is held by public opinion. During the past thirty years nearly three thousand Negroes have been lynched in various parts of the country. Scores have been burned alive at the stake. Even the bodies of women have been fed to the flames. Thousands of localities in various parts of the Union have experienced these outrages. A map of the United States with these localities indicated in blood spots would be a gruesome spectacle indeed. Our fair land of liberty is blotted over with these blood spots which cannot be washed out by all the waters of the ocean. It is not easy to calculate the total number of persons who have been involved in these lynchings, either as active participants, or as acquiescent lookers-on, every one of whom is a potential murderer, with the same guilt of conscience which Paul imparted to himself when he consented unto the death of Stephen. So general and widespread has become the practice that lynching may well be characterized as a national institution, to the eternal shame and disgrace of the land of the free and the home of the brave.

The practice of lynching is not influenced by the ascendancy of any political party. It prevailed with equal freedom under the administration of Harrison, Cleveland, McKinley, Roosevelt, Taft and Wilson. These American statesmen have all expressed their abhorrence of the practice, but have declared their impotence to deal with the evil. During the administration of President McKinley the riot in Wilmington, North Carolina, occurred. A horrible lynching took place in Alexandria, a few miles from the White House, which the President might have observed through his field glasses. The Atlanta riot occurred under the administration of President Roosevelt, the one great American who has an all-consuming passion for righteousness. But he was impotent to remedy by reason of the theory of government. The author had the privilege of introducing President Taft, who addressed the Alumni Association of Howard University on the subject of lynching.

He denounced the practice with all the ardor and indignation of his high-minded and generous nature, but there was not the slightest suggestion of an effective remedy through federal agency. Under the present administration, the burning at Waco, the automobile mob at Memphis, and the horrible outbreak at East St. Louis are still fresh in our memory, and have only been met with an expression of impotent regret. Grover Cleveland, with robust and untrammelled American spirit, was disposed to invoke the federal machinery to suppress local lawlessness, beyond any other President before or since his time.

We can hardly take up a daily newspaper without seeing startling headlines about Negroes lynched or burned at the stake. At first, it shocked and horrified the conscience, but according to the law of psychic economy, the public conscience has become so accustomed to these horrors as to be no longer shocked at their recurrence. I remember to have read in a great journal the description of a lynching in which it was stated that the victim was lynched, but that no cruelty was perpetrated. In truth and in deed,

"Vice is a monster of such frightful mien,
That to be hated, needs but to be seen;
Yet seen so oft, familiar to our face,
We first endure . . . then pity . . . then embrace."

The nation has allowed itself to become so accustomed to lynching that it has accepted it with complaisant toleration. The nation's conscience has become sere, and responds but feebly to the quickening power of moral appeal.

Lynching is not limited to the southern states, although it occurs more frequently there than elsewhere because of the relatively larger number of Negroes in the total population. There have been lynchings and burnings in Delaware, Pennsylvania, Ohio, Indiana, Illinois, Colorado, Kansas and other northern and western states. The evil is indeed national in range and scope.

Striking, indeed, is the analogy between the spread of lawlessness today and the spread of slavery two generations ago. Like slavery, lynching and lawlessness cannot be localized. Neither the evil nor the virtue of the nation can be held in airtight compartments, separating state from state, or section from section. As the nation could not exist half slave and half free under Abraham Lincoln a half century ago, so it cannot exist half law-abiding and half lawless today. The evil always tends to obscure the good, just as the darker phase overlaps the brighter in the waning moon. If the Negro is lynched in the South with impunity, he will soon be lynched in the North; so easy is the communicability of evil suggestion. The lynching of Negroes has become fashionable in some parts of the country, and is rapidly becoming fashionable in the nation at large. When a black man is accused of wrongdoing, "Lynch the Negro!" is the cry that springs spontaneously to the lips of man, woman and child. "Rape means rope," says the sententious Sam Jones. But the unlegalized rope has been the badge of ignominious death on the part of the black man only; just as the cross was the symbol of ignominy to be inflicted only on those who were not Roman citizens. If the institution of human slavery could have been separated and isolated in the South, it doubtless would have had a much longer lease of life. The Free Soil party sprang into existence not as a means of exterminating slavery, but for the purpose of keeping it out of the uncontaminated territory. But there could be no free soil in America unless all the soil were free. If lynching could be localized, the nation as a whole would have less pretext for interfering. But this cannot be done. Senator Tombs of Georgia boasted that he would call the roll of his slaves under the shadow of the Bunker Hill monument, an ambition which, doubtless, might have been gratified had not the nation arisen in its moral might and blotted out the iniquitous institution altogether. And so the Negro may yet be lynched, not only under the shadow of the Bunker Hill monument, but under the dome of the Capitol itself, unless the nation puts an effective stop to the evil practice.

Lynching cannot be confined to the Negro race. Hundreds of white men have been made the victims of summary violence. Although the Negro is at present the chief victim of lawlessness, yet, like any other disease, it cannot be limited by racial lines. The Jewish race has been made to feel the sting of race prejudice, culminating in the lynching of Leo Frank in Georgia, arousing the resentment of all Jewry at the deep damnation of his taking off. Italians were lynched in Louisiana, almost precipitating international controversy.

It is needless to attempt to place the blame on the helpless Negro. In the early stages of these outbreaks there was an attempt to fix an evil and lecherous reputation on the Negro as lying at the basis of lynching and lawlessness. Statistics most clearly refute this contention. The great majority of the outbreaks cannot even allege rapeful assault in extenuation. It is undoubtedly true that there are imbruited and lawless members of the Negro race, as there are of the white race, capable of committing any outrageous and hideous offence. The Negro possesses the imperfections of his status. As long as the race is held in general despite, just so long will it produce a disproportionate number of imperfect individuals of evil propensity. There are millions of Negroes who, like Topsy, "just growed."

They have missed the beneficent influence of home, school, church and society and cannot but show a lack of moral quality. It is folly to suppose that the neglected Negro, without the reinforcement of heredity, ennobling environment or formal education, will measure up to the highest standard of moral accountability. The white child with the advantage of heredity and environment must have his faculties carefully trained to meet the requirements of civilization. The Negro is susceptible to the ordinary influences that ennoble or degrade humanity. To relegate the Negro to a status that encourages the baser instincts, and then denounce him because he does not stand forth as a model of perfection, is of the same order of ironical cruelty as shown by the barbarous Teutons in Shakespeare's *Titus Andronicus* who cut off the hands and hacked out the tongue of the lovely Lavinia, and then upbraided her for not calling for perfumed water to wash her delicate hands. The Negro is neither angelic nor diabolical, but merely human, exemplifying the virtues and vices which belong to the status which he has been forced to occupy.

The Negro should be encouraged in all right directions to develop his best manly and human qualities. Who will say that he does not respond to humane treatment? The Negroes who have had the proper influences brought to bear upon their lives show as high a degree of conduct and manly demeanor as any other element of our population. When the black man deviates from the recognized standards of conduct he should be punished by due process of law, no whit augmented or abated because of his race identity. It is a fatuous philosophy that would resort to cruel and unusual punishment as a deterrent of crime. Lynching never made one Negro virtuous, nor implanted the seeds of right doing in the heart of any human being. On the other hand, it has lowered the sensitiveness of the conscience of the white race, and has damaged the moral reputation of the nation.

Lecherous assault cannot be proved to be an innate characteristic of the Negro. The practice is not uncommon among all civilized nations. The United States military authorities have recently hanged an American soldier in France for rapeful assault and murder. Violation of feminine chastity meets with as condign punishment in Africa as in civilized lands. During the days of slavery it was unheard of. In the midst of the Civil War, when the white men of the South left their fortunes and their families in the keeping of the black man whose chains they were endeavoring to tighten on the field of battle, he returned inviolate all that was committed to his care. In the West Indies, and, indeed, in the entire world range of race contact, this charge is not lodged as a peculiar characteristic of the Negro race.

LAWLESSNESS

The contact, adjustment and attrition of the various races of mankind constitute a problem which is coterminous with the ends of the earth. The lighter and stronger breeds of men are coming in contact with the darker and weaker ones. How does it happen that in the United States alone of all civilized lands, these atrocious outrages are heaped upon the helpless Negro? No other helpless people anywhere in the world have been made the victims of such lawlessness and outrage. The English nation has had the largest colonial experience and success of any peoples since the destruction of the Roman empire, and has come into relationship with the various weaker breeds of men in all parts of the world. But lynching never prevails under the British flag. In the West Indies, where the Negroes outnumber the whites 20 to 1, the word has not yet found place in the local vocabulary. In Brazil and other South American states, which are involved in a more complex racial situation than that in the United States of America, racial peace and good will prevail, and racial prejudice and passion are controlled and held in restraint. The United States enjoys the evil distinction, among civilized nations of the earth, of taking delight in the murder and burning of human beings. Nowhere else do men, women and children dance with ghoulish glee and fight for ghastly souvenirs of human flesh and mock the dying groans of the helpless victim, which sicken the air, while the flickering flames of the funereal pyre lighten the midnight sky with their dismal glare. The blood of the Negro cries from the ground unto the conscience of the nation.

The evil is, indeed, national. So must the remedy be. It is but hollow mockery of the Negro, when he is beaten and bruised and burned in all parts of the nation, and flees to the national government for asylum, to be denied relief on the ground of doubtful jurisdiction. The black man asks for justice and is given a theory of government. He asks for protection and is confronted with a scheme of governmental checks and balances. If democracy cannot control lawlessness, then democracy must be pronounced a failure. The old adage still holds true:

> "For forms of government let fools contest—
> Whatever's best administered—is best."

The nations of the world have a right to demand of us the working out in their integrity of our institutions at home before they are promulgated abroad. The outrages of which the Belgians so deeply and so justly complain are but merciful performances by gruesome comparison with these daily inflictions upon the American Negro. Our frantic wail against the barbarity of Turk upon Armenian, Russian against Jew, German against Belgian, are belied and made of no effect. It cannot be said that these outbreaks are but the spontaneous ebullitions of popular feeling, without governmental sanction or approval. They occur all over the nation and give it an evil reputation in the eyes of the world. Sins of permission are as reprehensible as sins of commission. A nation that permits evil practices to go unchecked and hides behind a theory of government is as reprehensible in the eyes of the world as the nation that assumes responsibility for them.

A few years ago a Turkish ambassador became *persona non grata* to the government for calling attention to the moral inconsistency of the United States in denouncing the outrages perpetrated by Turks upon Armenians, while condoning or ignoring those committed by whites upon blacks. The nation is compelled, in a spirit of humility, to accept the reproach which the world hurls into our teeth: "Thou hypocrite, first cast the beam out of thine own eye; and then shalt thou see clearly to cast the mote out of thy brother's eye." Every high-minded American must be touched with a tinge of shame when he contemplates that the rallying cry of the land of the free and the home of the brave is made a delusion and a snare by reason of racial barbarities. The world is at war with the Teutonic powers because the German government openly declared an international treaty to be a mere scrap of paper. But, long before this avowed declaration, the Fourteenth and Fifteenth Amendments—the vital parts of the Constitution of the United States—were made scraps of paper by the practice and condonation of the American people.

An outspoken governor of one of the states of the Union was widely denounced throughout the length and breadth of the land for saying: "To hell with the Constitution where the race issue is involved!" It was not the substance, but the unceremonial and explosive form of the utterance that evoked popular condonation. The nation cannot face its own conduct. It accepts the fact, but shrinks from the phrase. It, therefore, must blot out lynching and lawlessness in order to safeguard its moral reputation.

At Houston, Texas, a group of Negro soldiers, goaded to desperation by reflex racial passion, inflicted a heavy toll of fatality upon the whites, reversing the usual order of perpetrator and victim. The white race, accustomed to centuries of self-restraint and social control, swiftly overrides the exactions of civil and divine law in reaction to the virus of race passion. The Negro, in turn, made delirious by the same passion, overleaped the rigors of military discipline.

The American conscience has been touched and quickened by the East St. Louis and Houston outbreaks as it has never been before. Press and pulpit have tried to forget these outrages.

At each fresh outbreak they would lash themselves into a spasm of virtue and exhaust the entire vocabulary of denunciation, but, forthwith, would lapse into sudden silence and acquiescent guilt. By some fatuous delusion they seem to think that the atrocities of Springfield, Wilmington, Waco, Atlanta, Memphis and a thousand other places of evil report would never be repeated, nor the memory rise up to condemn the nation. But silence and neglect merely result in compounding atrocities. The East St. Louis and Houston occurrences convinced the nation, as it has never been convinced before, that the time for action has come. The press is not content with a single editorial ebullition, but, by repeated utterances, insists that the nation shall deal with its most malignant domestic evil. Reproach is cast upon the American contention for the democratization of the world in face of its lamentable failure at home. Ex-President Roosevelt has openly proclaimed, in a dramatic declaration, that these outbreaks make our moral propaganda for the liberation of mankind but a delusion and a snare. Can this nation hope to live and to grow in favor with God and man on the basis of a lie? A nation with a stultified conscience is a nation with stunted power.

Experience shows that there can be no effective reform of widespread evil by local or state authority. Slavery, long regarded as a local institution, could be destroyed only by the firm hand of the national government. Polygamy, traffic in vice, the white slave trade, prohibition, peonage and the divorce evil cannot be controlled by state action, but must be wiped out by an all-embracing federal law. Lawlessness and lynching are more insidious and widespread than any other national evils. They ramify throughout the entire nation, flourishing more abundantly in some sections and localities under fostering local conditions. This evil taints the national character and cries loudly for national remedy.

In time of war it is necessary to centralize authority in the hands of the federal government. The President, in the midst of the world war, has been given all but dictatorial powers. It is necessary to resort to autocratic methods in order to destroy hated autocracy. The federal government controls our common carriers and dictates what we shall eat and what we shall drink and what we shall or shall not say. All of this is justified on the basis of military necessity. But ample means to blot out lawlessness would be justified on the ground of moral necessity.

The United States has the largest percentage of murders and homicides, and the lowest average of legal executions, of any nation on the face of the earth. Ex-President Taft, in a notable address before the Civic Forum of New York City in 1908, stated that there had been 131,951 murders and homicides in the United States since 1885, and only 2,286 legal executions. In 1912 there were 9,152 homicides and 145 executions. The laxity of the law lies at the root of the evil. In a new country like ours, where pioneer conditions prevailed, and where the stronger race was confronted by two more primitive races, and where authority was subject to little or no legal constraint, the spirit of lawlessness survives long after the evoking conditions have passed away.

Pioneer conditions and the racial situation, in the earlier days, developed a sense of personal liberty and local freedom on the part of the white man which was intolerant of restraint even by the federal government. Robert Burns, committing the common logical fallacy of misconstruing an incidental circumstance into a casual relationship, in one of his frenzied outbursts, exclaimed: "Whisky and freedom go together." Subsequent experience has shown that they are as mutually antagonistic as evil and good. And they are not only unrelated, but, in the long run, one is destructive of the other. By parity of error, the wild spirit of lawlessness, which seems to flourish as a baytree in the boasted land of the free and home of the brave, might be disposed to insist that lynching and liberty go together. But the error is delusive and fatal. The principles are mutually destructive, like vice and virtue. The nation must destroy lawlessness or lawlessness will destroy the nation.

CHAPTER III

SEGREGATION

THE two races in America occupy separate social areas, with only incidental and temporary points of contact. In all purely personal and pleasureable relations of life, the two races are almost as distinct as if separated by interplanetary space. The races meet in matters of barter and business, but when these relations are released, each goes into his own company.

Under the old dispensation of master and slave, there was an understood overlapping area of social intimacy. A zone of social neutrality was established by complaisant condescension on the part of the whites and willing self-subordination on the part of the blacks. By domestic contact and familiarity the Negro was made an accepted member of the household and, under definitely understood limitations and restrictions, mingled with the whites on terms of social satisfaction. Much of the harshness and severity of slavery was relieved through such contact. Indeed, the advocate of slavery defended it as a patriarchal institution, where master and servant were bound together by satisfactory ties of mutual interest and kindly feeling. The inhuman barbarities of the system, such as were revealed in "Uncle Tom's Cabin," were exhibited mainly in the commercial aspect where the circle of ownership became too large to be covered by the personal contact of human sympathy of the master class, which had to rely for hired intermediaries upon overseers who neither understood nor felt the ennobling bond of human sympathy.

But the Emancipation Proclamation destroyed this patriarchal relationship, and overlapping circles of race association became tangential. The white man no longer feels disposed to indulge in any feat of social intimacy between the races, for this action would be construed into acceptance of social equality, whereas under the old dispensation no such construction was possible. It is related that a Russian nobleman, making a voyage to America, locked himself up in his cabin in complete social isolation from the other first class passengers, but that frequently he might be found on the lower deck indulging in free and easy intercourse with the steerage emigrants. On being questioned concerning his seemingly inconsistent attitude, he replied that social intimacy with his fellow cabin passengers might be easily misconstrued, while his friendly relationship with those in the steerage could not possibly be misunderstood.

The white race endeavors to separate the social spheres of the two races by a horizontal plane, keeping the lowest level of white life above the highest attainable aspiration of the Negro. Illustrating the different levels of the kingdoms of this world and the kingdom of heaven, Jesus states that John the Baptist was the greatest man born of woman, yet that the least in the kingdom of heaven was greater than he. By parity of illustration the white race might say that Booker T. Washington was the greatest man born of a Negro woman, yet the two relative spheres are so far apart that the least white man is greater than he.

In his famous Atlanta oration, Booker T. Washington laid the foundation of his fame upon a phrase describing the working of social relationship between the races. According to this philosophy, in all purely business and civic relations, the races might act together as the hand and yet remain separate as the fingers in social matters. The difficulty of the doctrine lies in the tendency of the social domain to enlarge itself so as to include the entire area of human relationship. Because the Negro must be kept socially apart from the white man, he is not allowed to work at the same trade, be domiciled in the same locality, attend the same school, ride in the same coach, worship in the same church or be buried in the same graveyard. Social affinity, which is essentially voluntary and spontaneous, transcends its proper sphere when it attempts to exclude those outside of the charmed circle from enjoyment of life, liberty and the pursuit of happiness.

During the last extra session of Congress, numerous bills were introduced by southern members for the purpose of segregating employés of the federal government. But under the guidance of wiser and more comprehensive leadership, such regulations were relegated to the pigeonhole of Congressional oblivion. Several southern cities enacted laws separating the residential areas of the two races, but such statutes have been nullified by a decision of the Supreme Court of the United States. The writer sat as an auditor in the Supreme Court when this case was being argued. It so happened that M. Vivian, Ex-Premier of France, member of the French High Commission sent from the democracy of France to make an appeal to the democracy of America, was a guest of the Chief Justice on this occasion. This gallant representative of the gallant French Republic was confronted by the ridiculous anomaly of witnessing the highest tribunal in the dominant democracy of the world trying to determine whether or not the rights of an American citizen at home to buy and occupy property should be limited by race and color. Great indeed was the triumph of democracy when a right decision was reached on this issue.

The effect of segregation would be to fix upon the American nation a caste system which human experience proves a blight to every civilization where it is allowed to take hold. Democracy is incompatible with caste. The federal statute books, so far, are free from race or class legislation. At the time of the founding of the Constitution, one-fifth of the population was of African blood and servile status. But the far-seeing wisdom of the founder omitted all racial designation or discrimination in the organic law. A government boasting of equality as its basic principle which should deliberately debase the weak and helpless among its own citizens would be an anomaly in the eyes of the nations of the earth. Amid all the passion and tumult of the anti-slavery conflict the federal statutes were kept free from the odium of race distinction. The *obiter dicta* importing race distinction into the decision of that tribunal were swiftly repudiated by the moral indignation of the aroused conscience of the American people. For this government, today, to declare that the Negro shall not enjoy identical rights and privileges with the rest of his fellow-citizens would be equivalent to the re-enactment of the discredited dogma of Judge Taney. Indeed, the principle involved is just as vital to the ideal of the nation today as it was sixty years ago, although the public conscience may be less keenly alive to it.

The war amendments to the Constitution reaffirmed the original intention—that there should be no race distinction recognized by the national government. These great amendments written into the Constitution by the point of the bayonet dipped in patriotic blood can never be erased nor their purpose ultimately defeated. Race discrimination is mentioned only to be forbidden. Mindful of the existence of these amendments, the states that have enacted laws repugnant to their spirit and letter, have sought circumvention by cunningly devised phrases and tricky contrivances. Every such revised constitution bears the stamp of righteous condemnation in its phraseology.

The American people for two generations have been divided in local alignment as to the relation of the Negro race to the federal government. The South has always been opposed to the recognition of the Negro as a federal citizen, and has striven incessantly to reduce him to governmental nullity. It would deny him both the right to vote and the privilege of holding office. Every southern senator voted to repeal the Fifteenth Amendment when that proposition was added as a rider to important legislation before Congress. No northern senator voted for this proposition, because it does not represent the spirit or purpose of his state or section. The policy of segregating the Negro is the outgrowth of the same local spirit. The leaders of southern thought and opinion do not hesitate on all occasions to declare their fixed and unalterable purpose to eliminate the Negro from all political and governmental consideration. The policy is well understood and accepted as the political dogma of that section.

In the duel for national supremacy between the North and South, during the generation preceding the Civil War, the South was hopelessly overmatched. Today it constitutes less than one-third of the population of the United States and has fallen far below its former rival in wealth, education and liberal ideas. This is in no sense a reflection upon the South, which has striven heroically to measure up to the standard of excellence set by the North, under severe and serious handicap. But it is a plain statement of palpable fact pertinent to the issue now under discussion. Massachusetts and Iowa, rather than Mississippi and Georgia, embody and typify the national spirit. The southern attitude on the race question has become provincial, while the northern position is national.

This race has all but universally favored and followed the part of the North. The anti-slavery crusade developed in the North against the pro-slavery obsession of the South; the one upheld the cause of liberty and union; the other was devoted to secession and slavery; the one imbibed the spirit of progress; the other, that of reaction; the one stood for the rights of man; the other, for the arrogance of race. The Negro's cause was caught up in the vortex of the whirlwind of patriotic fervor, sweeping from the higher latitudes and lashing itself against the barriers of the lower tiers of States. The party of the North rode triumphant on the storm, while the party of the South bore the brunt of its fury. Sections and parties for the time being became connotative, like up and down in ethics; the North was synonymous with patriotism; the South, with disloyalty. To the mind of the uncritical Negro, the North and the friends of the Negro race were one and inseparable in the advocacy of all of his political and civil rights, while the South and his enemies were united in the bonds of iniquity to antagonize his progress. And yet, the southern white man's attitude toward the political status of the Negro has always been determined by circumstances of racial situation rather than from any abstract theory of government. His political tenets are the outcome of circumstances and environment rather than of any inherent principle of party creed. The differentiating principle, which lies deeper than lines of political division, is that communities with heavy Negro population are hostile to political and civil equality, while those with thinly scattered numbers are either friendly or indifferent to that proposition. There is no psychological division of the white race determinative of the status of the black member within their midst.

It is imperative that the federal statutes should be forever free from race proscription, whatever afflicted states may feel forced to do under the pressure of acute issues. California, if unrestrained, might pass laws forbidding Japanese ownership of land in that state, but this would furnish no justification for the federal government to sanction or adopt such policy.

The policy of social separation of the races, alleged in justification of such measures, is a matter with which the federal government has nothing to do. The intimate social and personal relationship of citizens do not fall within the scope or purview of the federal authority. Its concern is with the comprehensive relations of all citizens. Matters of minor detail are left to local and subordinate jurisdictions.

The general government cannot find warrant for such action in the example of the several southern states. Discriminatory laws in the states are sought to be justified on the ground that the greater number of Negroes are unprepared for participation in government or for free intermingling with the whites without seriously lowering the tone and standard of civilization. The federal government has absolutely no such basis of excuse. The Negro represents at present less than eleven percent of the total population. This ratio is growing less with the passing of the decades. So far, no state with so slight a Negro element has deemed it necessary to adopt a code of "Jim Crow" laws. The federal government leaves each citizen socially where it finds him.

Those who advocate the policy of segregation permit themselves to indulge in the fallacy that it is for the best advantage of the Negro. It was once said that slavery was best for the Negro; later we heard that "Jim-Crow" cars were enacted especially for the benefit of the Negro; and then disfranchisement was intended for his well-being. It remains for some grim humorist to rise up and declare that lynching is encouraged for the black man's peculiar and especial benefit. It does seem strange that iniquitous practices, which are universally condemned by mankind, are regarded as for the best welfare of the Negro race.

When the Negro contends for public equality, he is often accused of the desire to force himself into association wherein he is not wanted. If this were his motive, the accusation would be justified. If Negroes walk on the north side of the street on a summer's afternoon, it is not because they desire to force association with whites who occupy the same thoroughfare, but they are both seeking shelter from the scorching rays of the burning sun, and the fact that they are thrown together is incidental to their common quest of the same advantage. When the Negro seeks a residence where white people happen to live, it is not that he wishes to force himself into unwelcome association. The whites, representing the more numerous and wealthy elements of the population, are apt to occupy the more advantageous localities and sections.

The Negro is in quest of a fair chance to work out his own destiny, and to contribute his share to the common honor and glory of the nation. This he cannot do if handicapped and circumscribed by laws separating him from the rest of his fellow men. Already handicapped by tradition and environment, it is poor sportsmanship on the part of his white fellow citizens still further to handicap him in the race of life. Equality of opportunity is the most that the Negro asks, and the least that a democratic nation can afford to grant.

CHAPTER IV

NEGRO PATRIOTISM AND DEVOTION

PATRIOTISM consists in the love of country, the love of home and of the local community. It is essentially an emotional attribute. The Negro is endowed with high emotional qualities which find outlet in outbursts of patriotic fervor. He possesses a sense of local attachment akin to that which the Jews manifested for beloved Zion. No sooner had the African captive forgotten the pang caused by violent severance from his native land than he fell in love with the land of his captivity. He early forgot the sunny clime and palmy wine of the native soil for the "cotton, corn and sweet potatoes" of Virginia. The transplanted Negro contributed the only original American music to the repertory of song. The city of Jerusalem and the region around about Jordan have become prototypes of the land of promise, merely because the humble people who lived there poured out their souls in joy and sorrow, expressing their patriotic attachment as transcending their chief joy. The Hebrew captive hung his harp upon a willow tree and refused to sing the songs of Zion in a strange land. But the transplanted African has glorified the land of his captivity by the songs of sorrow which sprang from his heart. These "spirituels" are but the expression of blind, half-conscious poetry, breaking through the aperture of sound before the intellect had time to formulate a definite cast of statement. The emotional element of patriotism is not manifested merely in epochs and episodes which produce renowned warriors and statesmen, but in the common deeds and endearments of the humble folk, which make the deepest impression upon the human memory and imagination. It is the folk song which manifests the folk soul.

The red Indian, the aboriginal owner of this country, has left no monument of enduring patriotism interpretable in terms of European thought and feeling. Anomalously enough, it was reserved to an Anglo-Saxon poet, Longfellow, to catch up the thread of the Indian's patriotic devotion in the legend of Hiawatha, and to the son of Africa, S. Coleridge Taylor, to give it musical expression. It is difficult to describe the current of feeling that flows through the soul of the speculative auditor as he listens to Negro voices in a choral rendition of Hiawatha, uttering with lyric pathos the patriotic soul of the red Indian, as portrayed by the Anglo-Saxon poet, and colored musically by the genius of the African composer.

Robert Burns, the national poet of Scotland, has seized upon the joys and sorrows, the deeds and endearments of the humblest cotters of that land, and woven them into soulful song which has made old Scotia ever dear to human memory and imagination. Who would not gladly go to the expense of a European trip in order to retrace the steps of the immortalized Tam O'Shanter, or to review the scene of Mary—poor, departed shade?

If human memory and imagination ever turn to our Southland with a passionate yearning for a manifestation of the outpouring of the human spirit, it will not be in quest of the deeds and doings of renowned warriors and statesmen, but rather in quest of the songs and sorrows and soul strivings of humble black folk embodied in plantation melodies. "Swanee River," "My Old Kentucky Home," and "Carry Me Back to Ole Virginny," spiritualize these regions beyond any other expression which they have yet evoked. Even the motif of the musical inspiration of the southern Confederacy, the world-renowned "Dixie," was but the embellishment of the expression of longing of a Negro for his homeland, where he was born "on an autumn day and a frosty morning." Which of America's patriotic songs would we not willingly exchange for "Swing Low, Sweet Chariot," or "Steal Away to Jesus"? There is no tone of bitterness in these songs. On the contrary, an undertone of love and devotion runs like a minor chord through them all. The plantation melodies which have come up from the low grounds of sorrow portray in sub-conscious form the patriotic as well as emotional capacity of this transplanted race.

They sometimes tell us that America is a white man's country. The statement is understandable in light of the fact that the white race constitutes nine-tenths of its population, and exerts the controlling influence over the various forms of material and substantial wealth and power. But this land belongs to the Negro as much as to any other, not only because he has helped redeem it from the wilderness by the energy of his arm, but because he has bathed it in his blood, watered it with his tears, and hallowed it with the yearnings of his soul.

The Negro's patriotism is vicarious and altruistic. It seems to be an anomaly of fate that the Negro, the man of all men who is held in despite, should stand out in conspicuous relief at every crisis of our national history. His blood offering is not for himself or for his race, but for his country. His blood flows like a stream through our national history, from Boston Commons to Carrizal. Crispus Attucks was the first American to give his blood as an earnest of American independence. His statue on Boston Common stands as a mute reminder of the vicarious virtues of a transplanted race. The Negro was with Washington in the dark days of Valley Forge, when the lamp of national liberty flickered almost to extinguishment. The black troops fought gallantly with Jackson behind the fleecy breastworks at New Orleans. Two hundred thousand black boys in blue responded to the call of the immortal Lincoln for the preservation of the Union. The Negro was the positive cause of the Civil War and the negative cause of the united nation with which we face the world today.

The reckless daring of Negro troops on San Juan hill marked the turning point in that struggle which drove the last vestige of Spanish power from the western world. The nation buried with grateful honor at Arlington cemetery the Negro soldiers who fell face forward while carrying the flag to the farthest point in the heart of Mexico, in quest of the bandit who dared place hostile foot on American soil. In complete harmony with this splendid patriotic record, it so happened that it was an American Negro who proved to be the first victim of ruthless submarine warfare after

President Wilson had distinctly announced to Germany that the continuance of such outrage would be considered tantamount to war. In all of these ways has the Negro shown, purposely or unconsciously, his undeviating association with the glory and honor of the nation. Greater love hath no man than this, that a man lay down his life for his country.

It is related that a Negro soldier was in hot-footed pursuit of a Mexican who had crossed the border line. The captain, noticing the pursuit, called a sharp retreat as the line of demarcation was approached. Upon his return, the captain said in a commendatory tone: "You certainly gave him a hot chase, but, you know, you must not cross the international boundary line." Thereupon the powder-colored son of thunder quickly responded: "Captain, if these Mexicans keep on fooling with us, we'll take up this international boundary line and carry it down to the Panama

Canal." This reply, so aptly spoken, expresses the attitude of every right minded Afro-American. Wherever the boundary line of American opportunity, privilege and prestige is to be flung, the American Negro will do his full share in pushing it thitherward.

The Negro's vicarious patriotism is but one form of manifestation of his vicarious nature. The devotion of the black mammy to the offspring of her mistress gives a new meaning and definition to that term. Out of the superabundance of her simple, unsophisticated soul she was able to satisfy the needs of the child of her heart, though not of her flesh, as nothing else could do. The man-slave, during the Civil War, in complete reversion of the law of self-interest, remained absolutely loyal to the family and fortune of his master, who at that very time was fighting to tighten the chains that bound him to lasting bondage.

Though not often proclaimed, it is a well known fact that several colored regiments enlisted under the banner of the Confederacy. Had the Richmond government carried out its tentative purpose to enlist Negro soldiers on a wholesale plan, there is little doubt but that colored soldiers would have followed the leadership of Lee as valiantly as they did that of Grant. This altruistic quality of loyalty and devotion is not destroyed by freedom and education, but translated and expressed in other terms.

Fifty years after the glorious victory at Appomattox, the lingering remnants of the boys in blue marched down Pennsylvania Avenue in the city of Washington, in semi-centennial celebration of that great event. There was not a dry eye on that Avenue, as white and black veterans, broken with the weight of years, marched with feeble tread to the reminiscent strains of friendly reunion: "Should Auld Acquaintance Be Forgot?" One year later the rapidly thinning ranks of those who followed the fortune of the

Confederacy marched down the same thoroughfare in celebration of their triumphant defeat. There was a noticeable intersprinkling of Negroes in their ranks also. The Negro's participation in these two parades epitomizes and expresses both his self-interested and his altruistic patriotism.

Ethnic character is too deep-rooted to be transformed by a political program. The Christ-like quality of long-suffering, forgiveness of spirit and loving-kindness is a natural coefficient of the Negro's nature. Booker Washington merely embodied and expressed the folk sense of his race when he said: "No man could be so mean as to make me hate him." The Negro, in the issue now upon us, will not sulk in his tent, nursing his grievances, like Achilles before the walls of Troy. He has no quarrel with the Germans. But he is fighting at the behest of his country. It is not to be wondered at if the German government, supposing that the Negro holds animosity and resentment with the stubbornness of the Teuton, should judge that he might furnish a fertile field in which to sow the seed of traitorous disloyalty. But such seed falls on stony ground. There is no depth of earth in the Negro's nature for its nourishment. The Negro will not deny or belittle his just grievances. He simply holds them in abeyance until the war is ended.

If it be a political as it is a sacred principle that without the shedding of blood there is no remission of sins, when we consider the blood of the African captive making red the Atlantic Ocean on his way to cruel bondage, the blood of the slave drawn by the lash, the blood of the black soldier shed in behalf of his country, we can say with Kipling: "If blood be the price of liberty, Lord God! the Negro has paid in full."

At such a time as this, when the national life and honor are involved in the prevailing struggle, the government must make careful appraisement of all available resources of both men and material. Mind power, man power and money power are the indispensable elements of success. The Negro, constituting one-tenth of the population, may be relied upon to contribute more than his quota of man power. There need not be the slightest apprehension concerning his loyalty, soldierly efficiency or willingness to serve his country. The Negro is sometimes called the Afro-American, and classified etymologically with the hyphenated citizens. But no hyphen separates his loyalty from that of his white fellow citizens.

The Negro's patriotism is an innate and spontaneous feeling. The race is endowed with emotional qualities which find outlet in an outburst of patriotic fervor. Strains of martial music and the Stars and Stripes floating on the breeze quicken his ardor and awaken his militant spirit. He does not stop to reason why, but is willing to follow the flag even unto death. He has also an attachment for locality which is the very essence of patriotism. He has hallowed the land of his enslavement by the sorrow songs that gushed from his heart. There is no tone of bitterness, but an undertone of love and devotion runs as a minor chord through it all.

"To the victor belong the spoils" is a righteous and just motto if the spoils be liberty. Those who fight for the honor and glory of the flag are worthy of a full measure of freedom and privilege under that flag. No right-minded American will care to dispute this proposition, and none will dare refute it. The reverse of this proposition is also true. No class that refuses to defend the flag in the hour of peril has any just claim to its protection in time of peace. The present war is a struggle for democracy; for the uplifting and ennoblement of the man farthest down. Racial and religious barriers are being swept away. Christian and heathen, Catholic and Protestant, Jew and Gentile, Asiatic and European, African and Aryan are all involved in one titanic struggle for freedom and humanity.

The world is engulfed in the red ruin of war. The present conflict is not due to the inherent deviltry of one nation or the innate goodness of the other. The cumulative ethical energies of society for generations have been damned up by barriers of hatred and greed. They seek outlet through the easiest crevice. The stored-up power is now breaking through the barrier as a cataclysmic convulsion of nations. The foundations of social order are being undermined by the shocks of doom. As an outcome of the war, the re-adjustment of the social structure will be more radical than that effected by the French Revolution. The transforming effect upon the status of the Negro will be scarcely less momentous than that produced by the Emancipation Proclamation.

The democratization of the world, coined as a fitting phrase, will be translated into actuality. The Declaration of Independence, penned by a slaveholder, sounded the death knell of slavery, although three quarters of a century elapsed between promise and fulfilment. The democratization of the world is but a restatement of this doctrine in terms of the present day. Political autocracy and racial autocracy will be buried in the same grave. The divine right of kings and the divine right of race will suffer a common fate. Hereafter no nation, however strong, will be permitted to override a weaker neighbor by sheer dominance of power; and no race will be permitted to impose an unjust and ruthless *régime* upon the weaker breeds of men through assumption of race superiority.

The people of all lands who are

heavy laden and overborne will be the chief beneficiaries of this war. The Negro problem is involved in the problem of humanity. The whole is greater than any of its parts. The Negro will share in the general momentum imparted to social welfare.

The Negro has been politically disfranchised in the South and industrially disfranchised in the North. Already he has been admitted to industrial opportunity in the North with manifest reflex action upon the harsh *régime* in the South. National prohibition, which is borne forward on the wave of the world war, will immensely improve his moral status.

Thousands of Negroes have been enlisted, and seven hundred Negroes have been commissioned as officers in the army of the United States. A Negro has been made assistant cabinet officer whose function is to adjust harmoniously the race's relation to the impending struggle. The improved attitude of the white race towards the

Negro is apparent in two affirmative decisions rendered by the Supreme Court of the United States with unanimous concurrence.

The Negro will emerge from this war with a redoubled portion of privilege and opportunity. The Negro will be loyal and patriotic, despite injustices and discriminations which try his soul. If he prevails, these trials and tribulations will work out a more exceeding weight of advantage. But if he allows them to overcome him, woeful will be his lot indeed! To stand sulkily by in resentful aloofness would be of the same kind of folly as to refuse to help extinguish a conflagration which threatens the destruction of one's native city, because he has a complaint against the fire department. The Negro will help put out the conflagration which threatens the world, and thus make the world his lasting debtor. He will stand shoulder to shoulder with his white fellow citizens to fight for the freedom of the world outside of our own national circle, and then hold them to moral consistency of maintaining a just and equitable *régime* inside of that circle.

The tide of democracy is sweeping through the world like a mighty river. Race problems and social ills are as marshes, backwaters, stagnant pools, estuaries, which have been shut off from free circulation with the main current. But the freshet of freedom is now overflowing its bed and purifying all the stagnant waters in its onward sweep to the ocean of human liberty and brotherhood, bearing upon its beneficent bosom all those who labor and are overborne.

CHAPTER V

RIGHTEOUSNESS

THE presence of the weaker race in the midst of a stronger is apt to develop the evil propensities on the part of the stronger. The same moral code is not applied to the weaker race. The ancient limitation of ethics which includes in its ennobling bond only one's neighbor is made to apply. Ethics takes on ethnic quality. Herein consists the inherent nature of the evil growing out of the contact of divergent races. Man is always prone to justify his unrighteous deeds by claiming that the object of his despite does not belong to the same ethical *régime* as himself. This is the attitude which the Jew is wont to exhibit toward the Gentile, rich toward poor, white toward black. All of the discrimination against the Negro rests on this basis. He was brought to this country as a slave because he was not considered of the same moral order as the white man. He is disfranchised and segregated and lynched for the same reason.

The supremacy of science rests upon the inexorability of natural law which pays no heed to the prejudices and predilections of man. The law of gravitation and the binomial theorem apply with absolute impartiality to all men, everywhere and at all times. They admit of no ethnic variation to accommodate human arrogance or caprice. By those who understand the principles of these laws, the prediction of their outcome may be relied upon with undeviating certainty. According to the foundation of Christian ethics, moral principles are as absolute in nature as natural law. The Ten Commandments, the Sermon on the Mount and the Golden Rule are as universal and impartial in their operation as the fixed principle in natural or physical science. Just as we could have no science of chemistry if the atoms could be made to obey one law to suit the racial pretensions of the Germans, and another to suit the Japanese, so our moral scheme is frustrated where the same formula is interpreted according to the manner of man to which it is to be applied.

A double standard in morals is as dangerous as a double standard in mathematics. A democracy that deals in double standards for its citizens is doomed. Identity is the essence of equality in all public functions. Two non-interchangeable parts cannot long maintain their original parity. There cannot be a different standard of weights and measures for the two races. A double yardstick would be an abomination to common sense. Although a sagacious statesmanship might decree that the two yardsticks should have the same length, and that the racial pounds should have the same weight, under the imperfections of human nature the Negro would soon be receiving the shorter measure and the lighter weight. If there were two standards of coinage of the same weight and fineness for the two races, provided only that one set should for ever circulate among Negroes and the other among whites, the black man's coinage would immediately depreciate in value. Parity can only be maintained by free interchangeability. The criterion of a standard of value consists of its easy currency and universal acceptance. The merchant who has one set of prices for the Negro and another for his white customers is considered dishonest. The physician who would treat his white patient according to one formula and his Negro patient with the same ailment according to another would violate the integrity of the science of therapeutics. The double moral standard of which the Negro is made the victim is manifest in the white man's general attitude towards him. To mistreat a Negro is not deemed a violation of the moral code. Even to kill a Negro is not considered a serious offence on the part of the white man in many sections of the country. So general has become this attitude and practice that the governor of a southern state in a notable proclamation stated that the open season for killing Negroes has closed in his state. Of the thousands and scores of thousands of Negroes who have been murdered in the South, few indeed are the instances where the perpetrator has been brought to justice. But where the race relation is reversed and the Negro kills a white man, condign punishment is swift and sure. That murder is murder by whomever committed ought to be an axiomatic assertion. But in actual experience murder is not murder where the perpetrator is white and the victim is black.

The impression which this attitude

leaves on the mind of the Negro is obvious. He is forced to feel that he is a moral alien, and is not considered a part of the ennobling bond of human sympathy. It would seem that enlightened self-interest on the part of the white race would lead them to hold up to the Negro the beneficent meaning and purpose of the law through its just and impartial enforcement. This is the practice of the English government in dealing with the natives in its colonies. In Bermuda and Jamaica the Negro swears absolutely by the integrity of British law, because it is enforced impartially on white and black alike, without the slightest suggestion of a double standard. But the Negro in the South no longer expects the impartial enforcement of the law where the feelings and passion of the white race are involved; and, consequently, he is led to look upon the law not as an instrument for preserving justice between man and man, but as a device for keeping him in subjection and subordination to the white race. The Negro appeals to the white man to enforce his own law. It is a poor sportsman who will not play the game according to the rules, especially when he makes the rules. The white man boasts of his God-given right to rule, but he should prove his right to rule by ruling right.

A nation that would endure must base its conduct upon the law of Righteousness. Moral grandeur is more enduring than material exploitation. A nation, like an individual, that walketh uprightly, walketh securely, because the centre of gravity falls inside the basis of support. Without fixed moral purpose, a nation, like a pyramid resting on its apex, is in unstable equilibrium.

Abraham Lincoln possessed the clearest understanding of any American statesman before or since his time. He was one of the few moral geniuses of the human race. He had an unclouded vision of moral values and an intuitive conception of ethical relationships. Our great national savior told us that this nation was conceived in liberty and dedicated to the proposition that all men are created equal. A nation that falls below the level of its fundamental ideals and goes in quest of false idols cannot hope to escape the fate of all apostate peoples of whom history makes record. God has given to America the moral opportunity to become the leader among the nations of the world along the line of national rectitude. Great will be its condemnation if, for any reason, it fails to live up to this great opportunity.

Moral reforms grow out of the people who suffer and stand in need of them. All of the moral progress of the race has been due to the circumstances and conditions of the humble and the lowly. God has chosen the humble things of life to confound the mighty. The whole course of American history has been given moral trend and direction by reason of the presence of the despised, neglected and rejected Negro. The Revolutionary statesmen, at a time when the question of African slavery had hardly become a keen moral issue, endeavored to ignore cognizance of the presence of the Negro. His unfortunate status, however, could not be obliterated in their subconsciousness, and so he seriously influenced the laws and statutes of that day. Like the victim who tries to conceal the gnawings of a vital disease, they affected to ignore the grievous evil which they inwardly felt. Thomas Jefferson, the great statesman of that epoch, said that when he contemplated the institution of African slavery he trembled for his country, feeling assured that God's justice could not sleep for ever. The Declaration of Independence and the Constitution of the United States made no avowed reference to the presence of the African, although, at the time, he constituted one-fifth of the total population. It was clearly in the minds of the far-seeing founders of this nation that, through some process of self-purification which they could not fully divine, American institutions ultimately would exemplify the principle of Righteousness for all men amenable to their control. They laid the foundation upon the bedrock principles of equality and justice, feeling that future generations would build upon no foundation other than that which they had laid.

The principles of the Declaration of Independence led to disquietude of the national conscience over the issue of African slavery. The leaven of liberty worked the nation into a moral ferment, which resulted in the Civil War and the emancipation of the slave. This was the greatest moral victory which the nation has ever achieved over itself. The triumph was universal and complete. African slavery, at first accepted with complacency by the Christian conscience, became quickened into a moral issue by a few minds of keener ethical discernment, and plunged the nation into fratricidal strife over a question of right and wrong. The right prevailed. The proponents of the lost cause now congratulate themselves over their defeat, while erroneously espousing the wrong side of a moral issue. By unanimous concurrence the nation has accepted the principle of Righteousness so far as human slavery is concerned.

We are not yet far enough removed from the prejudices and passions of that moral revolution to appraise justly or appreciate fully its influence and effect upon the nation's character. It is the one outstanding epochal event in our national life upon which all of the people can look with unalloyed satisfaction. When the kindly propitiation of time shall have completely obliterated the memory of the pangs of the awful divisive issues of that titanic struggle, the culmination of the quickening of the American conscience will be set forth in dramatic portrayal. John Brown will be the hero. Garrison, Grant, Lee and Lincoln will play important rôles. Ossawatomie and Gettysburg and Appomattox will be available for scenery and situation. The scene of the crowning act will be set at Harper's Ferry. Here nature piled the surrounding mountains as a fitting background. The blue skies of West Virginia shall be the uplifted curtain, while the confluent waters of the Potomac and Shenandoah shall represent the flood of tears that the nation will shed at the pity and pathos of it all. John Brown on the scaffold, pouring out his life for a race alien in blood and culture to his own, illustrates the highest point of moral sublimity that this planet has witnessed since Jesus Christ hung on the Cross. That scaffold is both the antetype and prototype of the moral history of America.

The Civil War marked the highest

practical expression of the national conscience. It required the Thirteenth and Fourteenth and Fifteenth Amendments to make our Constitution a charter of liberty indeed. All of this was brought to pass because of the presence and helpless condition of the Negro in our midst. Every modification of state or national constitution that has been made involving the complaint of the Negro has been in the direction of righteousness and moral grandeur. On the other hand, every alteration that has been made in local institutions limiting the just rights of the Negro has been contrary to the principles of Righteousness and has led ultimately to the reproach of those enacting them. Posterity will take no pride in the deeds of this day which deprive the humblest citizen of his human rights in order that others may enjoy a larger measure of easement.

Righteousness means more to the weak than it does to the strong. The strong nation may, for a time, seem to succeed in violation of the principle of Righteousness. It may be carried forward by an already acquired momentum, but the weak have no other reliance. We praise the sheep for his supposedly moral qualities of meekness, humility and forgiveness of spirit. We denounce the wolf for his savagery and ferocity of disposition. And yet, if we could analyze the workings of the minds of the two according to an exact psychological test, the sheep would be found to be no whit superior in inherent moral quality and essence to the wolf. He is just as cruel and exacting over all creatures with whom he has the advantage as the wolf is over him. They both follow the law of nature, in total oblivion of the law of Righteousness. But since the sheep is the weaker animal and the inevitable victim in the contest, we ascribe to him the moral advantage.

When Belgium felt she was a powerful land, she, through her monarch, laid violent hand upon a far-off African region and inflicted a ruthless *régime* upon the natives of the Congo, an act which brought down upon her head the moral condemnation of the civilized world. But, on a day, a stronger power laid a ruthless hand upon Belgium, and transformed her strength unto weakness, and, in her helpless and pitiful plight, she now appeals to the moral sympathy and support of the world.

The Jewish race throughout its history stood constantly in need of vicarious political salvation, and was thus enabled to teach the world the need of a vicarious spiritual Savior. Nations, like individuals, are prone to follow the law of nature, and rely upon the dominance of power until checked by a superior power. It is then that the weaker power invokes the beneficence of ethical consideration. The basic complaint against the German people lies in the fact that they are boastfully exploiting their acknowledged superior military efficiency over weaker nations without heed to the moral law. It is interesting to note the parallelism of argument of the German philosophers who justify their ruthless dominance over weaker European peoples, and that of our American publicists who strive to justify the lordship of the white man over the Negro.

Righteousness, like money, has an inherent value and a relative value. A coin has a fixed value, according to its weight and fineness, which means just as much to Mr. John D. Rockefeller as to the humblest washerwoman. But, relatively, it means immensely more to the washerwoman who may be dependent upon it to pay her weekly rental than it does to Mr. Rockefeller, in comparison to whose wealth it is a negligible quantity. So it is with moral qualities. While they have inherent and intrinsic values, yet they mean most to the people who stand mostly in need of them.

The Negro today stands mostly in need of the principles of public Righteousness because of his humble situation. But, as a compensation, this gives him the moral advantage and makes him the monitor over the conscience of the white race. Is it not an anomaly that the black man, who, throughout recent history, has not been noted for the higher and finer moral qualities and feelings, should stand as a monitor over the conscience of the white race, and have that claim allowed? The Negro says to the white race: "You ought to enact just and righteous laws and enforce them righteously." He says further: "You ought to apply the principles of Jesus, Whom you profess to follow, to your brother in black the same as to your brother in white." The white race is forced to plead guilty.

It is not contended that the Negro is inherently better than the white race. If he represented nine-tenths of the population and had the advantage of culture and opportunity and control of the machinery of public and practical power, it is not declared, although it is devoutly hoped, that he would be better in his treatment of the white race than the white race is at present in its treatment of him. But circumstances not only alter cases; they alter character. The Negro has the character and quality of his circumstances, which at present put him in the position of moral advantage whereby he makes appeal to the conscience of the nation in behalf of personal and public rectitude.

An individual or a nation is justly adjudged cowardly which will not exercise the full measure of its power to enforce its just and righteous demands. It is unjust to the wrongdoer to permit him to continue unrestrained in the perpetration of evil deeds. But where power is lacking, resort must be had to the higher ethical principles.

It may be said without blasphemy that the Negro is the only American who, as a class, can conscientiously utter the petition in Our Lord's Prayer: "Forgive us our trespasses as we forgive those who trespass against us." His long-suffering and non-resentful nature would readily forgive the white race all of its historical and contemporary trespasses, enormous as they are, if it would now accord him the consideration and human treatment which the law of human charity demands.

Some one has said: "No man is great unless he is great to his valet." No American statesman can attain transcendent greatness unless it rests upon the broad principles of Righteousness which meet the approval of all of the people, even the despised and rejected Negro.

Negroes all over this nation are aroused as they have never been before. It is not the wild hysterics of the hour, but a determined purpose that this country shall be made a safe place for American citizens of whatever color in which to live and work and enjoy the fruits of happiness. Ten thousand speechless men and women marched in silent array down Fifth Avenue in New York City as a spectral demonstration against the wrongs and cruelties heaped upon the race. Negro women all over the nation have appointed a day of prayer in order that Righteousness may be done to this people. The weaker sex of the weaker race are praying that God may invoke the great American conscience as the instrument of His will to promote the cause of human freedom at home and abroad.

At one of the six o'clock prayer meetings in the city of Washington, two thousand humble women snatched the early hours of the morning before going to their daily tasks to resort to the house of prayer. They literally performed unto the Lord the burden of their prayer and song, "Steal Away to Jesus." There was not a note of bitterness or denunciation throughout the session of prayer. They prayed as their mothers prayed in the darker days gone by, that God would deliver the race. May it not be that these despised and rejected daughters of a despised and rejected race shall yet lead the world to its knees in acknowledgment of some controlling power outside of the machinations of man? To one sitting there, listening in reverent silence to these two thousand voices as they sang,—

"On Christ, the Solid Rock, I stand,
All other ground is sinking sand—"

there could not but come the thought of this ungodly war which is now convulsing the world—a war in which Christian hands are dyed in Christian blood. It must cause the Prince of Peace to groan as in His dying agony when He gave up the Ghost on the Cross. The professed followers of the Meek and Lowly One, with heathen heart, are putting their trust in reeking tube and iron shard. As God uses the humbler things of life to confound the mighty, it may be that these helpless victims of cruelty and outrage shall bring an apostate world back to God. The Negro's helpless position may yet bring America to a realizing sense that Righteousness exalteth a nation, but sin is a reproach to any people.

THE END

PRINTED IN THE UNITED STATES OF AMERICA

LIBRARY
FLORISSANT VALLEY COMMUNITY COLLEGE
ST. LOUIS, MO.

AUG 1 1 1976

INVENTORY 74

FALL 76

INVENTORY 1983